Original title:
Mapping Melodies

Author: Oliver Bennett
ISBN HARDBACK: 978-9916-90-680-4
ISBN PAPERBACK: 978-9916-90-681-1

The Music of the Mind

In shadows soft, the whispers play,
A melody that guides the way.
Each thought a note, a gentle sound,
In silence deep, lost dreams are found.

Echoes dance on fragile air,
With secrets held, beyond compare.
Rhythms rise and fall like tides,
In quiet corners, the heart confides.

Harmonies of hope ignite,
Beneath the stars, in endless night.
The mind's vast stage, a grand ballet,
Where memories twirl and softly sway.

In every heart, a symphony,
Of laughter, love, and reverie.
A world unseen, yet understood,
The music of the mind is good.

Vivid Verses

Colors dance in the light,
Whispers of a bright delight.
Nature paints with strokes so bold,
Stories in hues yet untold.

Leaves flutter in a gentle breeze,
Taking flight from ancient trees.
Every shade a tale unfolds,
In the warmth of sunlit gold.

Rhythmic Reflections

Softly echoes in the night,
Steps that move without a fright.
Every heartbeat finds its way,
In the rhythm of today.

Sound of laughter fills the air,
Moments lived with love and care.
A dance of joy where shadows play,
In the music of the day.

The Strums of Space

Guitars hum in cosmic thrill,
Notes that linger, time stands still.
Stars aligned in perfect tune,
Underneath the silver moon.

Waves of sound across the skies,
Melodies that rise and rise.
In the vastness, dreams take flight,
Through the echoes of the night.

Melodies of Memory

Faded photos in a frame,
Each one whispers a sweet name.
Memories linger, hearts will soar,
In the songs we can't ignore.

Time may pass but love stays near,
Melodies that we hold dear.
In the silence, voices blend,
Through the tunes that never end.

Waves of Whimsy

A gentle breeze sweeps by,
Carrying laughter through the sky.
Waves of color dance and play,
Chasing the dull grey away.

In the shimmer of the light,
Dreams take flight, hearts feel bright.
Wanders lost in a daydream's fold,
Stories of wonder quietly told.

Each moment, a ripple we trace,
In the fabric of time and space.
Joyous giggles weave the thread,
In this tapestry we've spread.

As twilight drapes its velvet shawl,
Whimsy whispers, beckons us all.
Through starlit paths, we tread anew,
In waves of whimsy, just me and you.

The Anomaly of Ambiance

In shadows where silence clings,
An echo dances, softly sings.
Murmurs rise like misty streams,
Disrupting the calm of our dreams.

Colors clash, a fleeting fight,
Beneath the muted, fading light.
Anomaly brews in the air,
A strange familiarity, rare.

Each heartbeat pulses to a beat,
A rhythm twisted, bittersweet.
Moments flicker in twilight's haze,
Leaving traces of unspent days.

In odd harmony, we reside,
With whispers and shadows as our guide.
The ambiance swirls, enveloping whole,
A curious tug at the soul's scroll.

Cadence in the Clouds

Floating softly on the wind,
Where every thought is light-skinned.
Clouds compose a symphonic play,
In the vast sky, they drift and sway.

A lullaby of muted tones,
Cradles dreams, stirs ancient bones.
Each fluff, a gentle, whispered sound,
Where magic and silence abound.

Beneath this vaulted, azure dome,
Wandering hearts find their true home.
In sunlit beats and shadows grand,
We dance upon the soft, white land.

The cadence calls, we rise, we fall,
In rhythm with the heavens' call.
As we float through this endless blue,
A melody born in clouds, anew.

Resounding Revelations

In the quiet of the night,
Secrets whisper, taking flight.
Revelations break like dawn,
Illuminating paths we've drawn.

Memories echo in the still,
Filling hearts with flickers, thrill.
Each truth unveiled, a spark ignites,
Guiding dreams through starry nights.

In revelations deep and wide,
We find the courage to confide.
Chasing shadows of the past,
Discovering light that will last.

Resounding truths, they intertwine,
In the dance of fate and time.
Through every fear, through every pain,
Revelations flow like summer rain.

The Lyrical Quest

In shadows deep where whispers dwell,
A melody begins to swell.
With steps in time, we chase the light,
Through every note, we take to flight.

Each lyric penned in quill and ink,
A bridge to worlds, we dare to think.
Unfolding dreams in every rhyme,
A quest that bends the hands of time.

Soundscapes of the Soul

In quiet woods where echoes blend,
The heart's soft song begins to mend.
Among the trees, a tranquil chord,
In nature’s arms, our spirits soar.

The rustling leaves like whispered sighs,
A symphony beneath the skies.
Each breeze that passes brings a gift,
In harmony, our souls uplift.

Crescendos of Connection

When voices rise in joyful dance,
A tapestry of hearts' romance.
Each note a thread, each chord a bond,
In every space, we feel beyond.

The laughter shared, the tears that flow,
In crescendos, our spirits glow.
Through music’s pulse, we intertwine,
In every beat, our souls align.

Tracks of Tranquility

Along the path where silence breathes,
The gentle flow of dreams weaves.
In every step, a still embrace,
The world recedes, we find our place.

As rivers speak to distant shores,
In tranquil waves, our spirit soars.
With nature's hush, we find the key,
In quietude, we come to be.

Lyrical Latitude

In the whispering wind, dreams take flight,
Colors of dusk paint the fading light.
Hearts beat softly, a gentle refrain,
Echoes of hope, like drops of rain.

Underneath the stars, we find our way,
Guided by shadows that dance and sway.
With every heartbeat, a story unfolds,
Lyrical whispers, more precious than gold.

Echoes of Existence

In the stillness, existence calls,
Reflections linger within these walls.
Time flows slowly, a river of grace,
Each moment captured, a sacred space.

Faint echoes swirl in the evening air,
Memories linger, but do we dare?
To embrace the unknown, to keep it near,
Echoes of existence, haunting yet clear.

The Sound of Infinity

In the silence, infinity hums,
A cosmic dance as the universe drums.
Stars sing softly, a celestial choir,
Awakening dreams, igniting desire.

The rhythm of life, in cycles we weave,
Moments fade, yet we still believe.
In every heartbeat, a story divine,
Resonating whispers, the sound of infinity.

Harmonizing the Heartbeat

In the cadence of life, our souls align,
Melodies linger, an echoing sign.
Through joy and sorrow, we find our way,
Harmonizing heartbeats, come what may.

Like rivers flowing, together we rise,
Chasing the sunset, beneath painted skies.
In the symphony of existence, we stand,
Harmonizing the heartbeat, hand in hand.

Nature's Notations

Whispers of wind through trees,
Dancing shadows, gentle leaves.
Sunlight kisses the warm ground,
Nature sings without a sound.

Rivers flow with soothing grace,
Mountains hold a sacred place.
Birds take flight on vibrant wings,
In their songs, the wild heart sings.

Clouds drift softly in the blue,
Painting dreams in every hue.
Fields of gold sway with the breeze,
Nature's notes, a sweet reprise.

As the day fades into night,
Stars awaken, soft and bright.
In the silence, peace descends,
Nature's love, it never ends.

Notes from the Nebula

Cosmic whispers in the dark,
Stars ignite with a fierce spark.
Galaxies in dance, they twirl,
A silent song, the heavens swirl.

Time and space begin to bend,
Gravity, the universe's friend.
Waves of light blend with the night,
In the void, there shines a light.

Crimson hues and azure skies,
In the vacuum, starlight lies.
Nebulae in vibrant flight,
Charting dreams through endless night.

Echoes from the edge of time,
Celestial rhythms, pure and prime.
Infinite realms beyond our reach,
In their beauty, worlds they teach.

The Sound Map Unfolds

Silent footsteps on the ground,
Heartbeats echo, lost yet found.
Nature scribes her own refrain,
Every whisper, every strain.

Waves crash loud against the shore,
Wind chimes sing, a distant roar.
Rustling leaves tell tales untold,
In their flutter, magic unfolds.

Mountains hum a timeless tune,
Underneath the silver moon.
Every stone and flowing stream,
Part of life’s eternal dream.

In the quiet, sound can bloom,
Creating art within the gloom.
The sound map written through the years,
Plays in harmony, calms our fears.

Harmonies in Every Direction

Morning light breaks through the night,
Birds take wing, a joyful flight.
Nature’s chorus rises clear,
Harmonies that calm our fear.

Fields of flowers, colors blend,
Together as they sway and bend.
Bees humming sweet melodies,
In the breeze, life’s symphonies.

Mountaintops echo with delight,
In the shadows, whispers light.
Every sound, both soft and bold,
Weaves a story to be told.

From the ocean's rhythmic waves,
To the valley's secret caves,
Harmonies in every way,
Nature’s gift, our hearts' ballet.

Rhythms of the Untamed

In shadows deep, where wild hearts roam,
The echo sings a song untamed.
With every beat, the forest breathes,
In whispering winds, the rhythm weaves.

Through tangled roots and starlit skies,
The pulse of life begins to rise.
A dance of spirits, fierce and free,
In nature's embrace, we're meant to be.

The rustling leaves join in the fun,
A symphony beneath the sun.
In harmony with earth's soft grace,
We lose ourselves in this wild space.

Rhythms flow like rivers wide,
In this untamed world, we bide.
With every step, we find our way,
In nature's song, we choose to stay.

Chasing the Celestial Notes

Beneath the moon, the stars align,
They whisper secrets, oh so fine.
With every twinkle, dreams take flight,
Chasing the notes that dance in night.

A melody of dreams we sing,
Across the cosmos, light takes wing.
In melodies of distant stars,
Our hearts unite, no matter how far.

The universe holds endless tunes,
In twilight's grasp, beneath soft moons.
We reach for sounds that guide our souls,
Through gentle waves, our spirit rolls.

Chasing the notes of cosmic grace,
In every heartbeat, we find our place.
With spirits soaring, we'll explore,
The songs of silence, forevermore.

Navigating Through Chords

In strings of dreams, our fingers play,
Each note a map, guiding the way.
With rhythms bold, we chart the course,
Through ups and downs, we find the force.

Navigating life's sweet refrain,
In every chord, joy mixes with pain.
With harmony, we bind our fate,
Creating sounds that resonate.

The echoes ring, both near and far,
In every strum, we find a star.
Through minor keys and major ties,
Our spirits rise, while silence sighs.

Together we'll compose our song,
In shared vibrations, we belong.
Navigating through this vast expanse,
In chords of hope, we find our dance.

The Topography of Tone

In valleys low and peaks that soar,
The soundscape stretches, evermore.
With every rise and every fall,
The topography of tone calls.

From whispered winds to thunder's roar,
We traverse landscapes rich in lore.
In every echo, stories dwell,
In tones that rise, they weave and swell.

The map of sound is vast and wide,
With melody as our faithful guide.
Through cliffs of joy, and rivers deep,
In harmony, the world we keep.

With every note, we carve our path,
In the topography of sound, we laugh.
Together, through this journey roam,
In the landscape of tone, we find our home.

The Geography of Ghost Notes

In the quiet of the night, they play,
Whispers linger where shadows sway.
A melody wrapped in silken air,
Fleeting echoes, soft and rare.

Maps created in trembling sound,
Each note a ghost that won’t be found.
In the silence, stories hide,
Of wandering tunes that coincide.

A rhythm born from faded time,
In corners where the lost hearts climb.
With every pulse, they come alive,
In dreams where reminiscence thrives.

Unearthly tracks on forgotten lanes,
Haunting trails through joy and pains.
In the geography of what’s unseen,
Desires linger, old and keen.

Echoes Beyond the Horizon

Waves crash softly on distant shores,
Carrying tales of ancient scores.
The sun dips low, its light a trace,
Whispers traveling in nature's grace.

In the twilight, sparks ignite,
Illuminating stars in flight.
Voices linger, soft and calling,
Through the void, their echoes falling.

Horizons stretch to realms unknown,
Where every thought has seeds sown.
In the distance, dreams collide,
With every heartbeat, worlds beside.

Beyond the borders, spirits dance,
Entwined in time, a fleeting chance.
Echoes whispering in the breeze,
Reminding us to hold our dreams.

Soundscapes Beneath the Stars

Underneath the velvet night,
A symphony of pure delight.
Crickets sing their soothing tune,
As the moon rises, bright and soon.

Whispers ride on gentle winds,
Carried softly where the night begins.
Each note a story, each chord a sigh,
Painting pictures in the sky.

Silence holds the sacred space,
Where melodies find their grace.
In the cosmos, sounds converge,
As starlight pulls the heart to surge.

In this vast and wondrous dome,
Each sound reminds us of our home.
Together with the cosmic lore,
We dance beneath the night once more.

The Journey of Vibrant Voices

In the chorus of the open air,
Voices rise, unbound, unfair.
Each tone a journey, bold and bright,
Leading us into the deepening night.

Woven stories, rich and loud,
Of dreams not lost within the crowd.
Every shout, a spark of fire,
Fueling hopes and wild desire.

Through valleys low and mountains high,
Our vibrant voices touch the sky.
In unity, we seek the truth,
Awakening the spirit of youth.

With every echo, we share our dreams,
Painting life in endless themes.
As we journey through the vibrant noise,
We find our strength in every voice.

The Atlas of Soundwaves

In the depths where echoes play,
Waves of whispers guide the way,
Every note, a fleeting trace,
Mapping sounds in time and space.

Rippling rhythms softly sway,
Harmonics dance, a bright ballet,
From the highs to sunken lows,
In their embrace, the silence grows.

Melodies weave through the air,
Carving paths of sonic care,
In the stillness, secrets blend,
Where every song finds its own end.

Together they paint the night,
Filling shadows with pure light,
An atlas drawn in vibrant hues,
Of soundwaves that always ensues.

Harmonious Horizons

A horizon brushed with sound,
Where all lost notes can be found,
Distant chimes and lullabies,
Breathe life into twilight skies.

Every whisper tells a tale,
On the tides where voices sail,
From the dawn to dusk's embrace,
Harmony finds its rightful place.

In the twilight's softest glow,
Vibrations linger, ebb, and flow,
Songs of warmth, where spirits rise,
In concert with the starlit skies.

To horizons wide and free,
We chase the notes of destiny,
In this symphony of dreams,
Life unravels at the seams.

A Compass of Cadences

In the quiet, beats resound,
Steering souls from lost to found,
Each rhythm, like a guiding star,
Leads us to where we are.

Cascading through the night,
Cadences glow, a soft light,
With each pulse, a journey starts,
Mapping paths within our hearts.

From the silence, whispers flow,
Echoes pulse, a constant show,
In every pause, we find our way,
Through the night, into the day.

This compass forged of sound and space,
Guides us tenderly with grace,
In each note, a promise sings,
Of freedom that the music brings.

The Sonorous Trail

On the trail where echoes roam,
Every step, a note finds home,
In the rustle of the trees,
Singing soft, a gentle breeze.

With each footfall, sound awakes,
Life is woven in the breaks,
Through the woods, the shadows sway,
In harmony, they dance and play.

Follow the path of sound so sweet,
Where the earth and voices meet,
In the whispers of the night,
Find the warmth of moonlight's light.

The sonorous trail unfolds,
In its embrace, the heart unfolds,
With every note, a journey starts,
In the music, we find our hearts.

Tones of the Twilight

In the hush of the eve,
Soft whispers unfold,
Colors blend in the sky,
Secrets silently told.

Stars begin to shimmer,
As shadows take flight,
The world spins in silence,
Embracing the night.

Crickets hum their chorus,
As the moon shines bright,
A melody of wonders,
Rests in tranquil light.

Dreams drift like petals,
On a gentle breeze,
In the arms of twilight,
Time pauses with ease.

Resonant Realms

In the heart of stillness,
Echoes softly play,
Fields of sound awaken,
With each passing day.

Mountains hum their stories,
Rivers weave their song,
In every note that lingers,
Is where we all belong.

The forest breathes a rhythm,
Each leaf dances free,
Nature's grand performance,
A symphony to see.

Whispers of the ocean,
Call across the years,
Resonant with longing,
The melody appears.

Melodious Musings

Thoughts drift like soft clouds,
In a vivid blue sky,
Capturing the echoes,
Of a sweet lullaby.

Each word like a raindrop,
Falls on eager ground,
Sowing seeds of longing,
In a world profound.

Harmonies of silence,
Paint the dusky air,
A canvas full of wonders,
Caught in moments rare.

With every gentle heartbeat,
The world sings along,
In this dance of musings,
We find where we belong.

A Journey Through Sound

Step into the rhythm,
Let the echoes guide,
Each note a new adventure,
With the stars beside.

A path of glowing melodies,
Leads us through the night,
Every sound a whisper,
Every pause feels right.

From the rustle of the leaves,
To the distant train's call,
In the tapestry of sound,
We discover our all.

In the symphony of moments,
Life unfolds its dream,
A journey through sound,
Where we learn to esteem.

The Sound of Serenity

Whispers of the gentle breeze,
A calming pulse through ancient trees.
Rippling waters soft and low,
In nature's arms, we find our flow.

Distant mountains stand so tall,
Echoes of serenity call.
Morning dew on tender grass,
Time drifts by, moments pass.

Birdsongs weave a tranquil thread,
In the quiet, dreams are spread.
Beneath the sky so vast and blue,
Peace unfolds, a gift anew.

Echoing Dreams

In twilight's veil, the shadows creep,
Whispers linger, secrets keep.
Stars flicker like thoughts at play,
Echoing dreams in soft decay.

Phantoms dance in silver light,
Guiding wishes into the night.
Hopes alight like fireflies,
Chasing glimmers in the skies.

With every breath, a story we weave,
In this tapestry, we believe.
Past and future intertwine,
In echoing dreams, we find our sign.

Lush Lullabies

The forest hums a gentle tune,
Crickets chirp beneath the moon.
Leaves rustle in a tender mime,
Lush lullabies mark the time.

Breezes carry sweet refrains,
Melodies through meadow lanes.
Flowers sway, a dance in green,
Nature's choir, calm and serene.

As night descends, the stars awake,
In whispered notes, the night we take.
Dreams embrace in soft delight,
Lush lullabies cradle the night.

The Music of the Wild

Rustling leaves in whispered chats,
The dance of nature, wild as bats.
Beating hearts in sync with ground,
In the wild, pure music found.

Roaring rivers, cascading falls,
Every echo, nature calls.
A symphony of life and breath,
In every moment, beyond death.

Creatures sing in vibrant hues,
Each note reflecting morning dew.
Together we share this endless song,
In the music of the wild, we belong.

The Melody of the Moonlight

In the night, the whispers glide,
Softly through the starry tide.
Moonbeams dance on silver streams,
Cradling all our gentle dreams.

An echo hums through the trees,
Beneath the night's embracing freeze.
Notes of nightingale entwine,
With the pulse of hearts divine.

Reflections shimmer on the lake,
With every swish, the world awakes.
A lullaby of love unfolds,
As secrets of the night are told.

In twilight's grip, we find our place,
A harmony in time and space.
The melody flows, forever true,
In moonlit realms where love renews.

Uncharted Rhythms

Across the sands of shifting time,
Beats emerge without a rhyme.
Footsteps chase the fleeting light,
In the echoes of the night.

Drums of nature softly call,
Reverberating through us all.
Heartbeats merge in wild embrace,
In the pulse of endless space.

Waves crash softly on the shore,
A symphony forevermore.
Each note a story left untold,
In the dance of the brave and bold.

Under stars that twinkle bright,
We lose ourselves in sheer delight.
Uncharted paths weave in and out,
In rhythms that weave dreams without doubt.

The Symphony of Shadows

In the dusk, shadows play along,
A silent dance, a muted song.
Figures waltz on twilight's edge,
As day departs, we take the pledge.

Flickers of light show the way,
Guiding us as night meets day.
In every heartbeat, softly cast,
A symphony of shadows vast.

Whispers linger on the breeze,
Secrets carried through the trees.
In the depth of silent night,
Hidden truths come into light.

Together we'll explore the dark,
With every heartbeat, every spark.
In shadow's arms, we'll gently sway,
Embracing night until the day.

Harmonizing Horizons

Where the sun greets the sea,
Horizons paint a tapestry.
Colors blend in vibrant hues,
As day breaks with wondrous views.

Clouds drift softly across the sky,
Carrying dreams that soar and fly.
The world awakens with a sigh,
In harmony, the spirits tie.

Mountains rise with strength and grace,
Holding time in their embrace.
Each horizon tells a story,
Of nature's vast, unyielding glory.

Together we'll chase the dawn,
With hopes reborn as night is gone.
In every hue, our spirits fuse,
Harmonizing with the morning's muse.

Notes in the Night

Whispers float in the cool air,
Stars twinkle like eyes in the dark.
Soft melodies dance without care,
In shadows, they leave their mark.

The moon hums a sweet refrain,
While crickets play a gentle tune.
Each heartbeat feels lighter than rain,
As silence cradles the night's boon.

Dreams flutter like notes on the breeze,
Carried afar to places unknown.
In this stillness, the mind finds ease,
A calm echo of the night's own.

From deep, the pulse of life sings,
In the fabric of night, we are woven.
In harmony, the heartstrings cling,
To the symphony of stars' token.

The Orchestra of the Open Road

Wheels hum softly on the ground,
Each mile a note in the air.
Freedom's song is all around,
Adventure waits, robust and fair.

With every turn, a new refrain,
Endless skies stretch far and wide.
The engine's roar is a sweet gain,
As we drift with the morning tide.

The horizon calls with whispers clear,
Inviting us to journey on.
The road unfolds without a fear,
Under the watch of the dawn.

Underneath the vast expanse,
Every highway holds a tale.
In the rhythm, we find our chance,
To follow dreams down the trail.

Soundwaves of the Spirit

In silence, echoes softly rise,
Rippling through the endless night.
Each thought, a spark that defies,
The boundaries that block the light.

Voices carry on the breeze,
Whispers of wisdom, calm and bright.
In stillness, the heart finds ease,
Awakening the inner sight.

Resonate with nature’s song,
Feel the beat of the earth's heart.
In rhythm, we all belong,
As one, we dance in our part.

From the depths, our spirits soar,
Boundless in the gentle flow.
With each wave, we crave for more,
In the silence, we grow and glow.

Harmonious Hues

In twilight's glow, the colors blend,
With strokes that whisper of the dawn.
Each hue a story, lines extend,
A canvas where dreams are drawn.

Sunset spills a golden light,
Painting skies in vibrant streams.
In shadows, the stars ignite,
While hope gathers in our dreams.

Nature sings in every shade,
From deep crimson to soft blue.
In every frame, a tale is laid,
Of life’s wonders, ever true.

Together we weave our tales,
In every brushstroke, a vow.
In harmonious colors, love prevails,
As moments etch the world’s brow.

The Interlude of the Infinite

In whispers soft, shadows twine,
Stars weave dreams, a sacred sign.
Moments linger, time stands still,
In this silence, hearts will fill.

Echoes dance, a cosmic song,
Notes of joy where we belong.
Each breath a thread in endless space,
Lost in wonder, we embrace.

Fleeting glances, eternity,
Every heartbeat, a symphony.
In this realm of light and shade,
Life's rich tapestry is laid.

Infinite paths, souls unite,
Through the darkness, into light.
Together we craft our fate,
In this moment, we create.

Cacophony of Colors

Brushes dance, a vibrant clash,
Red and blue, a brilliant flash.
Yellow whispers, green's embrace,
In chaos found, we find our place.

Swirls of life on canvas bold,
Stories painted, yet untold.
Each stroke a voice, a tale to sing,
In every shade, the joys we bring.

Fractured light, a rainbow’s song,
Echoes of where we belong.
Colors fight, yet blend with grace,
In every hue, a new face.

Cacophony in harmony,
Artistry's sweet symphony.
Life’s true palette, rich and wide,
In every splash, our hearts abide.

Harmonizing the Horizon

Sunrise kisses ocean's face,
Colors mingle, time and space.
Horizons blush in golden glow,
Whispers of the winds that flow.

Mountains rise, bold silhouettes,
Nature's stage where dreams beget.
Clouds drift softly, secrets share,
In this realm, we cease to care.

Seas reflect the sky at dusk,
In twilight’s grace, we place our trust.
Harmony of earth and tide,
In endless peace, together glide.

Through the night, stars light the way,
Guiding us as we sway,
Every heartbeat, a gentle song,
Harmonizing where we belong.

Vibrational Voyages

Waves of sound, a rhythmic flow,
Carried forth where dreamers go.
In vibrations, spirits rise,
Echoes of the universe, wise.

Journeys made on sonic seas,
Floating soft on soothing breeze.
Each note a spark, igniting fire,
In every chord, a soul's desire.

Melodies weave through time and space,
Carving paths in endless grace.
Together in this sacred dance,
Vibrational waves, we take our chance.

Exploring depths of the divine,
In resonance, our hearts align.
Every whisper, an open door,
Vibrational voyages, we explore.

Melodic Wayfinding

In twilight's glow, the notes arise,
They dance like dreams beneath the skies.
Through valleys deep, the whispers weave,
In every breath, the heart believes.

Soft echoes chase the fading light,
As melodies take flight in night.
A symphony of whispers near,
Guiding hearts where hopes appear.

With every step, the rhythm flows,
A gentle pulse where spirit grows.
In harmony, the world we find,
A path of love, forever kind.

Away we drift on waves of sound,
In music's arms, we're safely bound.
Through tangled roots and soaring trees,
A voyage swayed by silver keys.

A Journey Through Soundscapes

In every note, a story told,
Of sunlit days and nights of gold.
Each chord a map, each beat a sign,
Through sound's embrace, our hearts entwine.

Waves of warmth across the sea,
Unfolding dreams like canopies.
We wander paths where echoes play,
In symphonies that shape the day.

Rustling leaves and distant calls,
Music rises, then gently falls.
In every sound, a world unfolds,
With secrets held and wonders bold.

Footsteps light on time's own thread,
Through rhythmic trails, our souls are led.
We journey forth, hearts open wide,
In soundscapes rich, our dreams reside.

Resonance in Refrains

Echoes linger soft and sweet,
In familiar tones, our hearts meet.
The chorus rises, strong and clear,
Binding us with notes we hold dear.

In every phrase, a sacred space,
Where love and joy begin to trace.
Each refrain brings us closer still,
A bond that time cannot instill.

Through ups and downs, the music swells,
In whispered truths, a story tells.
With every year, our voices blend,
In pathways made, we find our mend.

Resonant hearts in harmony,
Crafting love's sweet symphony.
Together we sing, together we soar,
In refrains that echo forevermore.

Lyrical Landscapes

Amidst the hills where silence reigns,
A melody flows through gentle plains.
In every note, the earth responds,
In lyrical dreams, our spirit wanders.

With painted skies of dusk's embrace,
Each lyric holds a timeless grace.
Through forests deep, and rivers wide,
In whispers soft, our souls confide.

The rhythm pulses like the tide,
In nature's arms, we joyfully bide.
With crafted words and heartfelt song,
In landscapes lush, we'll sing along.

From valleys low to mountains high,
In harmony, we’ll touch the sky.
With every breath, our hearts create,
A world of dreams, our calm estate.

Tuning the Terrain

In fields where whispers dwell,
Nature's pulse beats clear.
The wind crafts gentle spells,
Inviting hearts to hear.

Horizon lines converge,
With colors bold and bright.
Beneath the sky's large urge,
Dreams take their faithful flight.

Mountains guard their truths,
In silence, strong and grand.
Each valley holds its youth,
A story softly planned.

The rivers sing their song,
In rhythms pure and free.
Tuning all that's wrong,
To harmony we plea.

Cadences of the Cosmos

Stars echo from afar,
In dances slow and grand.
The moon, our shining star,
Casts light on all the land.

Galaxies spin with grace,
In patterns yet unknown.
A cosmic vast embrace,
Where silence is the throne.

Each comet trails a line,
A fleeting spark of fate.
In this grand design,
Time moves without debate.

Melodies weave the night,
In chords of dark and light.
The universe takes flight,
In endless, pure delight.

The Harmonic Atlas

Maps drawn in sound and sight,
Guide footsteps through the year.
Every note ignites the night,
Bringing distant dreams near.

Cities pulse like a heart,
In rhythms felt so deep.
With every street a part,
Of secrets safe to keep.

Mountains hum a soft tune,
While forests breathe in peace.
Beneath the watchful moon,
Harmony's sweet release.

We navigate with care,
These melodies we find.
Chasing dreams through the air,
The language of the mind.

Resonance of Revealing Routes

The paths unveil their tales,
As secrets intertwine.
Footsteps echo like gales,
With fate that's yet benign.

Each turn spins worlds anew,
In colors warm and cool.
The journey speaks to you,
With every twist, a rule.

In shadows lie the signs,
Where whispers guide our way.
Resonance softly binds,
As night transforms to day.

So follow with your heart,
To where the road will lead.
In every end, a start,
For souls that soar and plead.

Anthems of the Uncharted

Beneath the stars, we dare to roam,
In shadows deep, we carve our home.
With whispers low and dreams so bright,
We sing our songs into the night.

Each step we take, a tale unfolds,
The wild unknown, our hearts it holds.
With courage fierce, we break the mold,
In every triumph, stories told.

Across the void, our spirits soar,
To lands unseen, we yearn for more.
With every heartbeat, we ignite,
Anthems echo in morning light.

Through trials faced and bonds we find,
Each path we tread, a thread entwined.
Together strong, we journey free,
Uncharted realms, just you and me.

Cadential Cartography

In maps of sound, the world we trace,
A melody in every space.
With notes that dance upon the air,
We weave a tale, in rhythm bare.

Each measure holds a story spun,
Through silken chords, our hearts are one.
A symphony of hopes and dreams,
In fleeting echoes, life redeems.

With every beat, we chart the course,
In tonal streams, we find our source.
As harmonies embrace the night,
Cadences spark with pure delight.

The map unfolds, our fate defined,
In every note, new worlds we find.
Through sound we soar, as souls unite,
In harmonious dance, our spirits light.

Exploration Through Sound

Awake the senses, hear the call,
In every sound, we break the wall.
With whispers soft and echoes bold,
Exploration through sound unfolds.

From gentle rain to roaring seas,
Each sound a story, carried in breeze.
In silence deep, we listen close,
In sounds of life, our spirits boast.

With every note, a new path's drawn,
In vibrant sound, the dawn is born.
To journeys vast, our hearts are bound,
In every whisper, wisdom found.

Through sound we wander, free and brave,
In melodies, we learn to crave.
Exploration, a vibrant chase,
In every echo, we find our place.

Serenades by the Shore

Upon the waves, the moonlight streams,
A lullaby that softly gleams.
With gentle tides that kiss the sand,
Serenades by the shore, so grand.

Each whisper of the ocean's sigh,
A melody beneath the sky.
In harmony, the night does sway,
As stars above begin to play.

With every swell, a tale we weave,
Of love and dreams that we believe.
In salty air, our hearts align,
Serenades of love divine.

As dawn approaches, colors blend,
In every note, our lives transcend.
The shore will hold our cherished song,
In serenades where we belong.

Serenade in Stripes

In the twilight where shadows play,
Colors dance in a bright ballet.
Stripes of light flicker, weave, and sway,
Painting dreams that softly stay.

Echoes laugh in the evening breeze,
Hints of magic in rustling leaves.
Every heartbeat seeks to please,
Lost in tunes that nature weaves.

The moon peeks out, a silver guide,
In the melody, secrets reside.
With every note, the world confides,
In this serenade, hearts abide.

A chorus rises with the night,
Stars join in, a stunning sight.
Together they sing, pure delight,
In stripes of joy, the soul takes flight.

Whispers through Wilderness

In the hush of the forest deep,
Every shadow has secrets to keep.
Whispers linger where willows weep,
Nature's pulse in silence we steep.

Footsteps tread on a mossy floor,
Echoing tales from days of yore.
Every rustle holds the lore,
Of ancient spirits who wander more.

Moonlight spills on a silver stream,
Drawing the heart into a dream.
Where reflections dance and gently gleam,
In wilderness, we find our theme.

A call to the brave, the soul's quest,
In the wild, we can find our rest.
Whispers guide us, a gentle jest,
In nature's arms, we are blessed.

Chords and Coordinates

Across the skies, melodies roam,
In every chord, we find a home.
Coordinates trace where hearts may comb,
Mapping journeys that lead to foam.

Strings vibrate with the pulse of life,
Harmony cuts through rush and strife.
Each note a compass, sharp as a knife,
Guiding souls through joy and rife.

The rhythm sways like ocean tides,
In every wave, the music hides.
With every beat, the world abides,
In perfect sync, as love resides.

In webs of sound, we intertwine,
Notes like stars in a grand design.
Together we soar, the perfect sign,
In chords and coordinates, we shine.

Melodic Pathways

Through the valleys, soft notes flow,
Carving paths where wildflowers grow.
With every step, our spirits glow,
In melodic pathways, we follow.

The gentle strum of a distant lute,
Calls forth dreams, sweet and acute.
In the rush of life, we find our root,
Dancing along, our hearts salute.

Every breeze carries echoes around,
In the stillness, pure beauty found.
Melodies rise from the sacred ground,
In this journey, our souls are bound.

As twilight falls, the songs unite,
Filling shadows with warm delight.
In paths of music, hearts take flight,
Melodic journeys last through the night.

Discovering Musical Cartography

Notes sketch the air so light,
Mapping dreams in the night.
Every chord a step we trace,
In this vast, melodic space.

Harmonies weave far and near,
Soundscapes drawn, crystal clear.
A symphony of lands unknown,
In the heart, the seeds are sown.

Rhythms guide our wayward feet,
In this journey, oh so sweet.
Melodies like rivers flow,
Through the valleys love will grow.

With each note, new worlds arise,
Underneath the starlit skies.
In this map of sound we find,
The essence of the heart, entwined.

Pathways of the Heartbeat

A soft pulse leads us on,
Through the dusk and the dawn.
Every beat a story shared,
In the silence, hearts declared.

With each thump, a feeling new,
Unfolding paths in shades of blue.
As we walk, the rhythm grows,
Guiding where the loving flows.

Side by side, our echoes blend,
In this dance that knows no end.
Heartbeat whispers, secrets spoken,
In our journey, bonds unbroken.

Together in this tender space,
Finding comfort, warm embrace.
Every step, a shared delight,
In the glow of love's own light.

Whispers in the Wind

Breezes sing of tales untold,
Secrets carried, soft and bold.
Rustling leaves with gentle grace,
In the air, we find our place.

Echoes dance on wings of chance,
Nature's breath, a sweet romance.
Every gust a voice we hear,
Promises woven, crystal clear.

Through the branches, whispers glide,
Stories of the world outside.
In the hush, we stand and feel,
The embrace of truths revealed.

Treading softly, hearts in sync,
In the silence, hearts do think.
Every sigh, a love letter,
In the wind, we are together.

Sailing on Melodic Currents

Beneath the waves, we set sail,
Riding notes on a gentle gale.
Every swell a tune to know,
In the depths, our spirits glow.

With the stars as our guide,
We drift on where dreams collide.
The ocean hums a vibrant song,
In its rhythm, we belong.

Harmony sways with the tide,
In this voyage, we confide.
Sailing forth on winds so free,
In this realm, just you and me.

The horizon calls, clear and bright,
Through the dawn and into night.
With each chord, we find our way,
In melodic currents, we shall stay.

Cartography of Sound

In whispers of the wind, a map is drawn,
Beats of the heart, a resonant dawn.
Notes drift like shadows, tracing the air,
Melodies linger, a silent prayer.

On strings of the night, stars gently sway,
Guiding our dreams, leading the way.
Each sound a marker, each silence a mile,
In this vast landscape, we find our style.

With echoes of laughter, rivers intertwine,
Voices like colors, richly combine.
In the canvas of night, sound paints our fate,
In harmony's arms, we learn to create.

Through valleys of vibration, we wander free,
Listening close to what’s meant to be.
In the cartography of sound, we belong,
Under the stars, forever in song.

Harmonies Unfolding

In the cradle of dawn, soft notes arise,
Melodies dance, reaching the skies.
Strings hum a story, whispers exchange,
In the heart of the moment, we feel the change.

Echoes of laughter twirl through the air,
Fading shadows, a gentle prayer.
As layers unravel, a tune is revealed,
In harmonies unfolding, our souls are healed.

The rhythm of life flows beneath our feet,
A cadence of heartbeat, steady and sweet.
Each note a promise, each chord a chance,
In this grand sonnet, we join the dance.

With every sunrise, new symphonies bloom,
Creating a space where dreams can zoom.
In the world of sound, we find our way,
In harmonies unfolding, we learn to play.

The Symphony of Spaces

In quiet corners, echoes reside,
A symphony of spaces, a boundless tide.
Walls absorb whispers, secrets they keep,
In the stillness of night, old memories seep.

Rooms filled with laughter, shadows that grow,
Notes filled with warmth, in twilight's glow.
Every crack and crevice, each beam and stair,
Sings the soft story of love in the air.

Between fleeting moments, connections arise,
The pulse of existence, a sweet surprise.
In the fabric of life, melodies weave,
The symphony of spaces, a heart to believe.

Through windows of time, sounds travel far,
Like light from a distant, guiding star.
In the embrace of silence, we find our grace,
In the symphony of spaces, we find our place.

Echoes Across the Canvas

Brush strokes of sound paint the night,
Echoes across the canvas, pure delight.
Each note a color, each silence a hue,
Crafting a portrait that feels so true.

In the gallery of life, music thrives,
Creating a rhythm where passion drives.
With every crescendo, new dreams ignite,
In echoes that shimmer, we take flight.

As whispers of twilight wrap around us tight,
We dance with shadows, lost in the light.
In the art of existence, we play our part,
Echoes across the canvas, a vibrant heart.

In the depths of our souls, the echoes reside,
Painting the moments we cannot hide.
In this masterpiece, we find our way,
In echoes across the canvas, forever we stay.

Harmonious Echoes

In the twilight's gentle glow,
Whispers dance upon the breeze.
Nature sings in softest tones,
Hearts unite with melodies.

Mountains call with ancient hymns,
Rivers flow with rhythmic grace.
Every leaf a note in time,
Harmony in nature's face.

Echoes fade yet linger on,
Filling silence with their bliss.
Moments shared and softly held,
In the quiet, love can kiss.

Together in this sacred space,
Every sound a tender thread.
Woven dreams of joy and peace,
In the echoes, hope is bred.

The Journey of the Senses

Eyes awaken to the dawn,
Colors burst in vibrant hues.
Fragrant blooms unfold their charms,
Nature speaks in fragrant clues.

The taste of rain upon the skin,
Sweetest drops of summer's kiss.
Touch the earth and feel its pulse,
Every heartbeat sings of bliss.

Sounds of laughter fill the air,
Whispers dance upon the tide.
A symphony of senses play,
In each moment, joy's our guide.

With each breath, the world unfolds,
A tapestry of pure delight.
We embark on this grand quest,
Life’s journey shining ever bright.

Symphony of the Seasons

Spring awakens with a sigh,
Blossoms bloom in soft embrace.
Summer sun ignites the sky,
Golden warmth in every place.

Autumn's brush paints leaves of fire,
Winds of change begin to blow.
Winter wraps the world in white,
Silence falls as soft as snow.

Each season plays its lovely part,
Nature's song, a soulful rhyme.
Together forming life’s great art,
In the dance of fleeting time.

We dance along through joy and pain,
Embracing all that life bestows.
In every note, a sweet refrain,
A symphony that ever flows.

The Song of Solitude

In the stillness, silence speaks,
Echoes of my thoughts arise.
Within the calm, my spirit seeks,
Whispers soft as starlit skies.

Time suspends, a gentle pause,
Mountains stand as sentinels.
In this space, I find my cause,
Voices harmonize in wells.

Moments linger, rich and deep,
Solitude's a sacred friend.
Within this stillness, secrets keep,
A journey where all paths transcend.

Here I find my truest self,
In the quiet, wisdom grows.
Embracing all, I choose to dwell,
In the song that solitude knows.

The Symphony of Silence

In the hush, the whispers play,
Soft echoes dance and sway.
Moonlight sings on tranquil seas,
In silence, hearts find ease.

Time stands still, a gentle breath,
In quietude, there's life and death.
Stars converse in muted glow,
A music only few may know.

Crisp leaves rustle, secrets shared,
In nature's arms, we are ensnared.
Every pause, a story told,
In silence, dreams unfold.

As night deepens, shadows blend,
A symphony that knows no end.
In every stillness, peace abides,
In this silence, love resides.

Notes Across the Horizon

Each dawn brings a brand new song,
Notes that rise where we belong.
Whispers from the skies above,
Harmonies of hope and love.

Waves crash down with rhythmic grace,
Nature plays in vast embrace.
Sunset glows in colors bright,
Painting melodies of light.

Far-off hills hold tunes untold,
With echoes sweet and bold.
The breeze carries each refrain,
A reminder of joy and pain.

As twilight falls, we listen close,
For in silence, we find our dose.
Each heartbeat adds to the score,
A symphony we can't ignore.

Rhythms of the Unseen

Invisible hands weave through time,
Crafting beats, subtle as rhyme.
The earth pulses with ancient lore,
A dance we hear but can't ignore.

Soft shadows sway, a phantom ballet,
In the quiet corners where dreams play.
Each moment, a ripple in the deep,
Whispers of secrets we long to keep.

The breeze carries tales unheard,
In every flurry, a hidden word.
Life's essence flows like a stream,
In rhythms unbroken, we dream.

So close your eyes, feel the beat,
In the stillness, life feels sweet.
In the unseen, we find our way,
Dancing to the tune of today.

Lyrical Landscapes

Across the hills, a song takes flight,
Painting horizons with pure delight.
Meadows sway in a silent hum,
Nature's choir calls us to come.

Mountains stand as timeless guards,
Each peak a verse, life’s regards.
In valleys rich, the stories grow,
With every breeze, we come to know.

Rivers sing as they weave and flow,
Crafting paths where dreams can go.
The earth dons a lyrical veil,
In every corner, tales prevail.

So journey forth through spaces wide,
With open hearts, let hope be your guide.
In lyrical landscapes, we belong,
Together, forever, in nature's song.

Trails of Tune

In whispers soft, the breezes call,
A melody that weaves through all.
With every step, a note takes flight,
Together in the dance of night.

The earth beneath our feet alive,
In rhythm, hearts begin to strive.
With every path, a song we trace,
In trails of tune, we find our place.

From hills to valleys, wild and free,
The notes of nature's symphony.
As stars above begin to glow,
We wander where the music flows.

In echoes rich, the memories stay,
In timeless tunes, we find our way.
Through every sound and every sigh,
We walk the trails where spirits fly.

Harmonia’s Journey

Across the sky, the colors blend,
In Harmonia's tale, the notes descend.
With every rise, a story told,
In shifting shades of blue and gold.

The rhythm of the waves, a guide,
In every motion, secrets hide.
A journey drawn on ink of night,
With starlit whispers, pure delight.

From mountains high to oceans deep,
In harmony, the world we keep.
The heartbeats blend, a gentle song,
In every place, where we belong.

Through valleys lush, past rivers wide,
With every note, we feel the tide.
Harmonia's journey, ours to take,
In every step, the dreams we make.

The Cartographer's Crescendo

Ink on parchment, the world unfurled,
In every line, a story swirled.
The cartographer's pen takes flight,
Crafting maps that sing of light.

With compass set, the heart will guide,
Each journey drawn with arms spread wide.
In valleys low and peaks so grand,
We find the keys to unexplored land.

The crescendo builds, a symphony,
Each contour sings of destiny.
With every stroke, a dream conceived,
In maps of wonder, we believe.

Through ancient woods and rivers flow,
In every corner, the truth we know.
The cartographer leads where we must go,
In every map, the tales will grow.

Annotated Harmonies

In margins wide, the notes are penned,
Annotated tales that never end.
With every phrase, a voice will rise,
In whispers soft, beneath the skies.

The pages turn, each harmony found,
In gentle strokes, our hopes abound.
A dance of letters, pure delight,
In annotated dreams of night.

With every verse, a journey starts,
Connecting souls and beating hearts.
The laughter's echo, the silent sigh,
In written notes, we learn to fly.

So pen your thoughts and let them flow,
In harmony, the worlds we know.
Through every line, we share and grow,
In annotated love, the truth will show.

The Map of Unheard Symphonies.

In whispering winds, secrets unfold,
Melodies dance, yet remain untold.
A canvas of silence painted in dreams,
The soul finds its voice in the softest themes.

Each note a step on a path unseen,
Carved from the echoes of what might have been.
Chasing the shadows where rhythms reside,
A journey of hearts where passions collide.

In stillness we hear the softest refrain,
A map to our spirits, beyond joy and pain.
Guiding us through the night's gentle embrace,
With every heart's beat, we find our own space.

Let symphonies rise from the depths of the night,
With every heartbeat, let dreams take their flight.
In the quiet moments, we'll forge our own path,
A map of emotions, a symphonic bath.

Harmonic Cartography

Lines on a page, a tale to unfold,
Each curve a whisper, a story retold.
In patterns of sound, we trace the divine,
Crafting our lives in each perfect line.

With compass in hand, we sketch out the score,
From valleys of silence to harmonies shore.
A journey through rhythms, a dance of the free,
In notes we discover who we're meant to be.

Unfolding the maps that lead us to light,
In every beat, there's a purpose so bright.
We travel through echoes of moments we've known,
In cartography's embrace, we are finally home.

With every crescendo, our hearts intertwine,
In harmonic landscapes, our spirits align.
We follow the melody wherever it goes,
In the map of our souls, true harmony grows.

Echoes of the Heart

In the still of the night, whispers awaken,
Soft echoes emerge from the dreams we've forsaken.
Every heartbeat a story, a note in the dark,
Illuminating shadows, igniting a spark.

Each sigh is a rhythm, a pulse from the core,
Resonating gently like waves on the shore.
In the depths of our being, where secrets reside,
The echoes of love cannot be denied.

As time weaves its tapestry, threads intertwine,
In echoes of laughter, in love's sacred shrine.
We cherish the moments that linger and grow,
In the heartbeat's echo, we find our own flow.

In the quiet reflections, the past meets the now,
In echoes of the heart, we learn to allow.
With every soft whisper, we gather the light,
In the harmonies of love, we know we are right.

The Soundtrack of Stars

In the shimmer of night, a symphony plays,
The stars wink in rhythm, guiding our ways.
Each twinkle a note in the vast, cosmic score,
With every heartbeat, we long for more.

Galaxies whirl in a dance so divine,
A soundtrack of light where our dreams intertwine.
We float through the cosmos on melodies bright,
In the music of starlight, we find our true sight.

As constellations weave tales of old,
In every bright whisper, new stories are told.
The universe spins with a grace so profound,
In the soundtrack of stars, our spirits are found.

In the vastness above, our hearts come alive,
To the rhythm of planets, together we strive.
With every new dawn, let the music persist,
In the soundtrack of stars, we forever exist.

Echoes Beneath the Canopy

Whispers through the leaves, soft and low,
Dancing shadows in the twilight glow.
Nature's chorus, a sacred song,
Echoes of ages, forever strong.

Beneath the boughs where the silence reigns,
Footsteps fade and the heart explains.
A breeze carries secrets, untold and wide,
In the forest's embrace, we seek to hide.

The rustling branches, a gentle sigh,
Moments captured as they drift by.
In the stillness, we find our peace,
Echoes beneath, where worries cease.

A symphony rests in the emerald dome,
Each note a thread that weaves us home.
Together we stand, as the daylight wanes,
Echoes beneath, where nature reigns.

Melodies in Motion

Rhythms pulse through the city streets,
Every footfall, a heartbeat that beats.
Colors blur as the world spins 'round,
Melodies rise, in chaos found.

Voices blend in a vibrant flow,
Stories whispered in the undertow.
Harmony dances in the neon light,
A symphony born from day into night.

In every corner, a note will play,
Creating magic in the fray.
Joy and sorrow mix and collide,
In the melodies where we abide.

As the sun sets, the music swells,
Echoes of laughter and solemn spells.
Every moment a chance to explore,
Melodies in motion, forever more.

Sonic Scenarios

In a world where sound paints the air,
Whispers of dreams, tender and rare.
Vibrations ripple through time and space,
Sonic scenarios in life’s embrace.

A distant thunder, a lover's call,
Each note carries, feeling small.
Under the surface, a current flows,
In melodies, the heart knows.

From the crackle of fire to the ocean's sigh,
Every sound invites us to fly.
Composed of moments like stardust scattered,
Sonic scenarios, where nothing's shattered.

In the symphony of existence, we find,
The echoes of souls, uniquely intertwined.
Capturing life in an endless song,
Sonic scenarios, where we belong.

The Voyage of Vibration

Set sail on waves of harmonic grace,
Riding the currents, we find our place.
With every swell, a new tale spins,
The voyage of vibration, where it begins.

In the heart of the ocean, deep and wide,
Undercurrents of melody, a mystical tide.
Whistles of wind and the crash of foam,
Through the rhythm, we journey home.

Stars shimmer gently, guiding the route,
Celestial echoes in concert shout.
The timbre of night, a comforting sound,
In the voyage of vibration, we are unbound.

As horizons stretch, possibilities bloom,
With each gentle wave, we escape our gloom.
Together we dance on this endless sea,
The voyage of vibration, wild and free.

Milton Keynes UK
Ingram Content Group UK Ltd.
UKHW021349011224
451618UK00023B/212

9 789916 906804